Dedication

This book is dedicated to The Holy Spirit, my Inspiration, and my Help.

Also, to my loving wife, Veronica. Her unwavering support has played a tremendous role in my life.

WORSHIPING GOD IN TIMES OF TRIALS AND TRIBULATIONS

Overcoming Challenges Through Worship

PREFACE

Life is filled with a tapestry of experiences, weaving together moments of joy and triumph with trials and tribulations. Our faith is often tested during these challenging times, and our relationship with God is brought into sharp focus.

"Worshiping God in Times of Trials and Tribulations" guides those seeking to strengthen their faith and deepen their connection with God in the face of adversity.

This book is a compilation of practical tips, biblical verses, prayers, and spiritual insights designed to provide comfort, guidance, and encouragement during life's most challenging moments. Through the pages of this book, you will explore the power of worship as a source of solace, resilience, and hope in times of hardship. You will be equipped with spiritual tools and resources to help you navigate through the storms of life and emerge with a renewed sense of strength and faith.

Drawing from a wealth of scriptural wisdom and personal experience, "Worshiping God in Times of Trials and Tribulations" offers a roadmap for maintaining a solid spiritual foundation in life's challenges. From memorizing and reciting Bible verses to engaging in daily prayer and reflection, you will learn how to deepen your faith, access divine guidance, and draw strength from the presence of God.

In addition to the practical tips, verses, and prayers, this book also provides activities, worksheets, and inspirational quotes to help you apply the concepts presented within its pages. These resources encourage you to develop a personal worship practice tailored to your unique needs and circumstances.

As you embark on your journey through "Worshiping God in Times of Trials and Tribulations," may you find solace, resilience, and inspiration in the power of worship, allowing God to guide and support you through life's most trying moments.

Be Blessed,
Andrew Mwema

Table of Contents

INTRODUCTION 7
Definition of Trials and Tribulations 8
Importance of Worshiping God During Difficult Times 10
Biblical Basis for Worshiping God in Times of Trials and
Tribulations 13
Chapter 1 17
UNDERSTANDING TRIALS AND TRIBULATIONS IN THE BIBLE 17
Understanding the Purpose of Trials and Tribulations in the Bible
.... 20
The Purpose of Trials and Tribulations 20
Lessons Learned from Trials and Tribulations 22
Explanation of The Role of Worship During Times of Trials and
Tribulations 23
Worship as a Source of Comfort and Strength 23
Worship as a Form of Gratitude and Praise 24
Worship as a Means of Transformation 25
Chapter 2 27
THE IMPORTANCE OF WORSHIPING GOD IN TIMES OF TRIALS AND
TRIBULATIONS 27
Benefits of Worshiping God During Difficult Times 28
Applying the Benefits of Worship During Difficult Times 30
Importance of Having a Worshiping Community During Times of
Trials and Tribulations 31
Chapter 3 35

WORSHIPING GOD IN TIMES OF TRIALS AND TRIBULATIONS 35

Understanding The Different Forms of Worship 35

Steps To Take To Worship During Trials And Tribulations 39

Tips on How to Continue Worshiping During Difficult Times 41

Chapter 4 45

BIBLICAL VERSES AND PRAYERS FOR WORSHIPING IN TIMES OF TRIALS AND TRIBULATIONS 45

Compilation of Prayers Related To Worshiping God During Difficult Times 50

Explanation of the Importance of Memorizing and Reciting These Verses and Prayers 55

Chapter 5 58

EMBRACING WORSHIP DURING DIFFICULT TIMES 58

Recap of the Importance of Worshiping God During Difficult Times: 58

Encouragement to Continue Worshiping God During Trials and Tribulations: 59

Final Thoughts and Recommendations: 59

Bonus Chapter 61

Inspirational Quotes Related to Worshiping God During Difficult Times 64

ABOUT THE AUTHOR 67

INTRODUCTION

Welcome to "Worshiping God in Times of Trials and Tribulations," a Book that explores the importance of worshiping during difficult times based on the teachings of the Bible.

Trials and tribulations are an inevitable part of life, and they can leave us feeling overwhelmed, stressed, and lost. However, as Christians, we have a powerful tool: worship. Worship is a way to express our love, gratitude, and faith in God. It is a powerful way to connect with God and find peace, comfort, and strength during difficult times.

This book aims to help you understand the importance of worshiping God during trials and tribulations and provide practical tips on worship during difficult times. We will explore the biblical examples of trials and tribulations and the role of worship during these times. We will also discuss the different forms of worship and how to incorporate them into our daily lives.

Furthermore, this book will provide a compilation of biblical verses and prayers related to worshiping God during trials and tribulations. These verses and prayers will help deepen your understanding of worship and provide the necessary tools to navigate difficult times.

This book will be a source of inspiration, comfort, and encouragement for you during difficult times. Please read through it with an open mind and heart and incorporate the teachings into your daily life. Remember, worship is a powerful tool that can help you overcome any trial or tribulation that comes your way.

Definition of Trials and Tribulations

Trials and tribulations are experiences or situations that challenge us in various ways, both physically and emotionally. Feelings of stress, anxiety, and uncertainty often accompany them. Different circumstances, including illness, loss of a loved one, financial difficulties, relationship problems, or natural disasters, can cause trials and tribulations.

In the context of the Bible, trials, and tribulations are events or circumstances that test the faith and endurance of believers. The Bible teaches that trials and tribulations are an inevitable part of life, and they serve to refine our character and strengthen our faith. James 1:2-4 states, "Consider it pure joy, my brothers and sisters, whenever you face trials of many kinds, because you know that the testing of your faith produces perseverance. Let perseverance finish its work so you may be mature and complete, not lacking anything."

Furthermore, the Bible teaches that trials and tribulations are not random events but are part of God's plan for our lives. Romans 8:28 states, "And we know that in all things God works for the good of those who love him, who have been called according to his purpose." This means that even amid trials and tribulations, we can trust that God is working for our good and that He will use our It's important to note that trials and tribulations can affect individuals differently. While some people may feel strengthened and empowered by difficult circumstances, others may feel weakened and discouraged. How we respond to trials and tribulations depends on various factors, including our personality, past experiences, support networks, and faith.

It's also important to recognize that trials and tribulations are not punishments from God. While some people may feel that they are being punished for their sins or mistakes, the Bible teaches that trials and tribulations are simply part of the human experience. As Jesus said in John 16:33, "In this world, you will have trouble. But take heart! I have overcome the world."

Worshiping God during trials and tribulations can help us navigate these challenges with faith and hope. It can provide comfort and connection with God, reminding us that we are not alone in our struggles. As we turn to worship, we can draw strength and encouragement from the promises of the Bible, knowing that God is with us and will never leave us.

In the following chapters of this book, we will explore how worship can help us during trials and tribulations. We will look at biblical examples of trials and tribulations, the importance of worshiping God during difficult times, and how to incorporate worship into our daily lives. This book will also provide a compilation of biblical verses and prayers related to worshiping God during trials and tribulations, providing comfort and encouragement.

Importance of Worshiping God During Difficult Times

Worshiping God during difficult times is essential for Christians. It helps us to connect with God and find strength, comfort, and hope amid trials and tribulations. Worshiping God during difficult times can allow us to maintain a positive attitude, cultivate gratitude, and deepen our faith.

Firstly, worshiping God during difficult times reminds us of God's goodness and faithfulness. We acknowledge God's sovereignty and power over all circumstances when we worship.

We remember that God is in control and working for our good, even when we cannot see it. This helps us to trust in God's plan and to remain hopeful, even in the face of adversity.

Secondly, worshiping God during difficult times helps us to maintain a positive attitude. It can be easy to become pessimistic during difficult times, but worshiping God helps us focus on our lives positive aspects. As we sing hymns, offer prayers of thanksgiving, and recite scripture, we are reminded of the blessings that God has given us. This helps us to cultivate gratitude and to see our circumstances in a more positive light.

Thirdly, worshiping God during difficult times can deepen our faith. Trials and tribulations can challenge our faith, but when we worship, we reaffirm our belief in God's love, power, and grace. We are reminded of the promises of the Bible and God's faithfulness to His people throughout history. This strengthens our faith and helps us trust God's plan, even when we do not understand it.

Moreover, worshiping God during difficult times can also help us experience peace and comfort. As we worship, we can tangibly experience God's presence. We can feel His love and comfort and be assured that we are not alone in our struggles. This can bring us peace that transcends our circumstances and help us face our challenges with courage and strength.

The Bible is full of examples of people who worshiped during difficult times. In the New Testament, the Apostle Paul wrote many of his letters from prison, yet he encouraged others to worship God and to be thankful in all circumstances. In his letter to the Philippians, Paul wrote, "Rejoice in the Lord always. I will say it again: Rejoice!" (Philippians 4:4). Paul understood the importance of worshiping God during difficult times. He knew it could bring comfort and strength to those suffering.

Furthermore, the Book of Psalms contains songs and worship prayers written during trials and tribulations. In Psalm 42, the psalmist wrote, "Why, my soul, are you downcast? Why so disturbed within me? Put your hope in God, for I will yet praise him, my Savior and my God" (Psalm 42:5). This psalm is a beautiful example of how worshiping God during difficult times can help us to find hope and comfort in Him.

In addition, the Book of Hebrews encourages us to continue to worship God, even when we face trials and tribulations. Hebrews 13:15 says, "Through Jesus, therefore, let us continually offer to God a sacrifice of praise—the fruit of lips that openly profess his name." This verse reminds us that worshiping God is a continual act of faith, even when we face difficult circumstances.

The Bible teaches Christians that worshiping God during difficult times is essential. It helps us to maintain a positive attitude, deepen our faith, and experience peace and comfort. As we face trials and tribulations in our lives, we can turn to worship as a source of strength and hope, just like the examples of Job, Paul, and the psalmist in the Bible.

Biblical Basis for Worshiping God in Times of Trials and Tribulations

The Bible provides a strong foundation for worshiping God during trials and tribulations. It teaches us that worshiping God during difficult times is not only important, but it is also a commandment of God. This section will explore the biblical basis for honoring God during trials and tribulations.

One of the primary reasons for worshiping God during difficult times is to acknowledge God's sovereignty and power over all circumstances. In the Book of Isaiah, God says, "I am the Lord, and there is no other; apart from me, there is no God. I will strengthen you, though you have not acknowledged me so that from the rising of the sun to the place of its setting, people may know there is none besides me. I am the Lord, and there is no other" (Isaiah 45:5-6). This passage reminds us that God controls all things and that we should turn to Him in worship, even during trials and tribulations.

Moreover, the Bible teaches us that worshiping during difficult times is a way to express our faith and trust in God. In the Book of Habakkuk, the prophet writes, "Though the fig tree does not bud, and there are no grapes on the vines, though the olive crop fails and the fields produce no food, though there are no sheep in pen and no cattle in the stalls, yet I will rejoice in the Lord, I will be joyful in God my Savior" (Habakkuk 3:17-18). This passage teaches us that even when we face difficult circumstances, we can still worship God and find joy in Him.

In addition, the Bible teaches us that worshiping during difficult times can bring us comfort and strength. In the Book of Psalms, the psalmist writes, "The Lord is my rock, my fortress, and my deliverer; my God is my rock, in whom I take refuge, my shield and the horn of my salvation, my stronghold" (Psalm 18:2). This verse reminds us that God is a source of strength and comfort during difficult times and that we can turn to Him in worship for help and guidance.

Furthermore, the Bible teaches us that worshiping during difficult times can help us to maintain a proper perspective on our circumstances. In the Book of Romans, the Apostle Paul writes, "And we know that in all things God works for the good of those who love him, who have been called according to his purpose" (Romans 8:28). This passage reminds us that God can use difficult circumstances for our good and that we should turn to Him in worship, even when we do not understand His plan.

Lastly, the Bible teaches us that worshiping during difficult times can bring us closer to God. In the Book of James, the author writes, "Draw near to God, and he will draw near to you" (James 4:8). This verse reminds us that as we worship God during difficult times, we can draw closer to Him and experience His presence more profoundly.

The biblical basis for worshiping in times of trials and tribulations is clear. The Bible teaches us that worshiping during difficult times is essential for acknowledging God's sovereignty, expressing our faith and trust in Him, finding comfort and strength, maintaining a proper perspective on our circumstances, and drawing closer to Him. As we face trials and tribulations, we can turn to worship to connect with God and find hope, peace, and joy in Him.

Chapter 1

UNDERSTANDING TRIALS AND TRIBULATIONS IN THE BIBLE

The Bible is a book that recounts the trials and tribulations of many individuals throughout history. These stories illustrate how people have faced physical and emotional challenges and have found a way to persevere through their faith in God. This chapter will explore some of the critical examples of trials and tribulations in the Bible and what they can teach us about our struggles.

One of the most well-known examples of trials and tribulations in the Bible is the story of Job. Job was wealthy with everything he could ever want, including a loving family and a successful career. However, one day God allowed Satan to test Job's faith by taking away all his possessions and health. Despite these terrible losses, Job refused to curse God and remained faithful. Ultimately, God restored Job's health and prosperity, and he was blessed with even more than he had before.

The story of Job teaches us several important lessons about trials and tribulations:

1. It shows that God allows problems to come into our lives to test our faith and build our character.
2. It reminds us that even in the darkest times, we can still trust God and remain faithful.
3. It illustrates that when we persevere through our trials, God can bless us with even more incredible blessings than we had before.

Another example of trials and tribulations in the Bible is the story of Joseph. Joseph was sold into slavery by his jealous brothers and taken to Egypt, where he was falsely accused of a crime and imprisoned. Despite these terrible circumstances, Joseph remained faithful to God and eventually became the second-in-command to the Pharaoh of Egypt. Through his wisdom and leadership, Joseph saved the people of Egypt from a devastating famine and reunited with his family.

The story of Joseph teaches us several important lessons about trials and tribulations:

1. It shows that God can use us to accomplish great things despite difficult circumstances.

2. It reminds us that God can turn our problems into blessings if we remain faithful and trust Him.
3. It illustrates that forgiveness and reconciliation are possible even in difficult situations.

The story of Moses is another example of trials and tribulations in the Bible. God chose Moses to lead the Israelites from slavery in Egypt and into the Promised Land. However, he faced many challenges, including the Pharaoh's resistance, the Israelites' lack of faith, and his doubts and fears. Moses remained faithful to God through it all and led the Israelites to freedom.

The story of Moses teaches us several important lessons about trials and tribulations:

1. It shows that God can use ordinary people to accomplish extraordinary things if we obey Him.
2. It reminds us that even when we face overwhelming obstacles, God can provide the strength and resources to overcome them.
3. It illustrates that trusting God and His plan can overcome our doubts and fears.

The trials and tribulations in the Bible teach us valuable lessons about faith, perseverance, and trust in God. Through the stories of Job, Joseph, and

Moses, we see that even in the darkest times, God is with us and can use our trials to build our character and accomplish great things. As we face our trials and tribulations, may we remember these lessons and trust God's plan for our lives.

Understanding the Purpose of Trials and Tribulations in the Bible

The Bible is filled with stories of people who faced trials and tribulations. From Job to Joseph, to Jesus Christ, and the Apostle Paul, the scriptures recount the stories of individuals who were challenged by adversity and emerged stronger and wiser. The purpose of these trials and tribulations is a central theme in the Bible, and understanding it can help us better appreciate the lessons that can be learned from these stories.

The Purpose of Trials and Tribulations

The purpose of trials and tribulations in the Bible is multifaceted. First and foremost, they serve to test and refine our faith. The Bible teaches us that trials and tribulations can help to strengthen our faith, and the perseverance we develop through them can produce good qualities in us. The Book of James says, "Consider it pure joy, my brothers and sisters, whenever you face trials of many kinds because you know that the testing of your faith produces perseverance" (James 1:2-3).

In addition to testing our faith, trials, and tribulations also serve as a means of correction and discipline. The Book of Hebrews states, "Endure hardship as discipline; God is treating you as his children. For what children are not disciplined by their father?" (Hebrews 12:7). Trials and tribulations can be seen as a form of discipline that helps to shape us into better individuals and followers of Christ.

Furthermore, trials and tribulations can be used to help us to grow in our character. The Bible teaches that adversity can produce patience, perseverance, and compassion. Romans 5:3-4, it says, "Not only so, but we also glory in our sufferings, because we know that suffering produces perseverance; perseverance, character; and character, hope."

Finally, trials and tribulations can be used to draw us closer to God. We can develop a deeper relationship with God through these difficult times and experience his love and grace more profoundly. In times of hardship, we may turn to God for strength, comfort, and guidance.

Lessons Learned from Trials and Tribulations

Through the stories of individuals who faced trials and tribulations in the Bible, we can learn valuable lessons about faith, perseverance, and character. For example, the challenges of Job teach us the importance of remaining faithful to God even in the face of great adversity. Despite losing his possessions, children, and health, Job remained steadfast in his faith and was ultimately rewarded by God.

Similarly, the story of Joseph teaches us the importance of trusting God's plan for our lives. Although he was sold into slavery by his brothers and faced many challenges, Joseph remained faithful to God and was eventually rewarded by becoming an influential leader in Egypt.

The story of Jesus Christ teaches us the importance of sacrificial love and obedience to God. Jesus faced persecution, rejection, and death on the cross but remained committed to redeeming humanity and reconciling us to God.

Trials and tribulations are a part of life, and the Bible teaches us that they can serve a valuable purpose in our spiritual growth and development. Through the examples of individuals who faced trials and tribulations in the Bible, we can learn valuable lessons about faith, perseverance, and character and emerge from adversity more robust and wiser. Whether we face physical, emotional, or spiritual challenges, we can trust God's plan and remain faithful, knowing he is always with us.

Explanation of The Role of Worship During Times of Trials and Tribulations

Worship is a central aspect of the Christian faith and is essential in times of trials and tribulations. In the Bible, we see numerous examples of people who turned to worship during difficult times, finding solace and strength in their connection with God. In this section, we will explore the role of worship during times of trials and tribulations in the Bible.

Worship as a Source of Comfort and Strength

During trials and tribulations, worship can serve as a source of comfort and strength for believers. When we worship, we focus on God and his goodness rather than our problems and struggles. In doing so, we are reminded of God's power and faithfulness and find renewed hope and courage to face whatever challenges come our way.

In the Book of Psalms, we see numerous examples of people who turned to worship in times of difficulty. Psalm 46:1-3 says, "God is our refuge and strength, an ever-present help in trouble. Therefore we will not fear, though the earth give way and the mountains fall into the heart of the sea, though its waters roar and foam and the mountains quake with their surging." This psalm reminds us that God is our refuge and strength and that we can find comfort and protection in him.

Similarly, in the New Testament, we see examples of believers who turned to worship during times of persecution and hardship. In the Book of Acts, the religious leaders arrested and threatened the apostles, but they continued to worship and proclaim the good news of Jesus Christ. Acts 5:41-42 says, "The apostles left the Sanhedrin, rejoicing because they had been counted worthy of suffering disgrace for the name. Day after day, in the temple courts and from house to house, they never stopped teaching and proclaiming the good news that Jesus is the Messiah."

Worship as a Form of Gratitude and Praise

In addition to being a source of comfort and strength, worship can also serve as a form of gratitude and praise during trials and tribulations.

Even amid arduous circumstances, we thank God for his blessings when we worship. This gratitude attitude can help shift our focus away from our problems and onto the goodness of God.

In the Book of Philippians, the apostle Paul encourages believers to cultivate gratitude and praise. In Philippians 4:4-7, he says, "Rejoice in the Lord always. I will say it again: Rejoice! Let your gentleness be evident to all. The Lord is near. Do not be anxious about anything, but in every situation, by prayer and petition, with thanksgiving, present your requests to God. And the peace of God, which transcends all understanding, will guard your hearts and minds in Christ Jesus." This passage reminds us that even during trials and tribulations, we can find peace and joy by turning to God in worship and thanksgiving.

Worship as a Means of Transformation

Finally, worship can also serve as a means of transformation during trials and tribulations. When we worship, we are transformed by the power of God's Spirit, becoming more like him in our thoughts, attitudes, and actions. Through worship, we are reminded of God's love and grace and inspired to live out our faith in tangible ways.

In the Book of Romans, the apostle Paul encourages believers to offer themselves as living sacrifices, holy and pleasing to God. In Romans 12:1-2, he says, "Therefore, I urge you, brothers and sisters, in view of God's mercy, to offer your bodies as a living sacrifice, holy and pleasing to God—this is your true and proper worship. Do not conform to the pattern of this world, but be transformed by the renewing of your mind. Then you will be able to test and approve what God's will is—his good, pleasing, and perfect will." This passage reminds us that worship is not just a matter of singing songs or saying prayers but a lifestyle of surrender and transformation.

Worship is central to the Christian faith and is imperative during trials and tribulations. We find comfort, strength, gratitude, and transformation when we worship in challenging times. Through worship, we are reminded of God's goodness and inspired to live out our faith in tangible ways. As we face trials and tribulations, let us turn to worship, knowing that God is with us and that we can find solace and strength in his presence.

Chapter 2

THE IMPORTANCE OF WORSHIPING GOD IN TIMES OF TRIALS AND TRIBULATIONS

Trials and tribulations are a part of life, and they can often leave us feeling overwhelmed, anxious, and alone. During these difficult times, it can be easy to lose sight of God's goodness and become consumed by our problems. However, the Bible teaches us that worship can play a crucial role in helping us to navigate through these challenging circumstances. Worship can provide comfort, strength, gratitude, and transformation in trials and tribulations. Whether facing physical, emotional, or spiritual challenges, let us turn to worship to find solace and strength, knowing that God is with us always.

In this chapter, we will explore the importance of worshiping in times of trials and tribulations, looking at examples from the Bible that show us how we can turn to God in worship, even in difficult circumstances.

Benefits of Worshiping God During Difficult Times

Worshiping God during difficult times can be a powerful spiritual and emotional well-being tool. Whether dealing with loss, illness, or personal struggles, worship can offer comfort, strength, and inspiration. This section will explore some of the benefits of worshiping during difficult times.

1. **Worship brings comfort and peace.**

One of the most significant benefits of worshiping during difficult times is the comfort and peace it can bring. When we worship, we focus away from our problems and toward God's presence and power. This can help us find a sense of calm and security, even amid the turmoil.

For example, when a loved one is sick or dying, worship can be a means of finding solace and strength. Finding peace of mind or heart can be challenging in these situations. However, worship can offer a respite from worry and anxiety, connecting us to God's love and care.

2. **Worship offers a means of expressing gratitude and praise**.

Another benefit of worshiping during difficult times is the opportunity to express gratitude and praise to God. We acknowledge God's goodness and faithfulness when worshipping, even in adversity. This can help us to maintain a positive attitude and focus on the blessings in our lives.

For example, when we face financial struggles or job loss, it can be easy to become discouraged or pessimistic. However, worship can remind us of the things we do have, such as family, friends, or our faith. We can maintain a positive outlook and remain hopeful by expressing gratitude and praise for these blessings.

3. **Worship can inspire transformation**.

Finally, worshiping God during difficult times can be a means of transformation in our lives. When we worship, we open ourselves to God's guidance and inspiration, allowing Him to work in our hearts and minds. This can inspire us to make positive changes and seek God's will for our circumstances.

For example, when we face personal struggles or addiction, worship can be a means of finding hope and strength. Turning to God in worship can inspire us to make positive changes, such as seeking help, setting boundaries, or developing healthier habits.

Applying the Benefits of Worship During Difficult Times

While the benefits of worship during difficult times are numerous, knowing how to apply them in our daily lives can be challenging. Here are some practical ways to incorporate worship into our lives during difficult times:

1. **Find a community of believers:** Worshiping with others can be a powerful way to connect with God and find support during difficult times. Consider joining a church or small group where you can worship with others and receive encouragement and prayer.
2. **Create a daily worship routine:** Set aside time daily to engage in worship, whether through prayer, reading the Bible, or singing worship songs. This helps establish a daily routine and brings a sense of consistency and stability during difficult times.
3. **Seek out worship resources:** Many resources are available to help us worship during difficult

times, such as worship music, devotionals, or online worship services. Consider utilizing these resources to enhance your worship experience and connect with God deeper.

4. **Practice gratitude**: Expressing gratitude can be a powerful way to shift our focus away from our problems and toward God's blessings. Consider starting a gratitude journal or taking time each day to reflect on what you are thankful for.

5. **Lean on God for strength**: Remember that worship is about expressing gratitude, finding comfort, and leaning on God for strength and guidance. Pray for God's wisdom, help navigate challenging circumstances, and trust in His plan for your life.

Worshiping during difficult times can offer numerous benefits, from comfort and peace to transformation and inspiration. We can find hope and joy despite adversity by incorporating worship into our daily lives and leaning on God for strength and guidance.

Importance of Having a Worshiping Community During Times of Trials and Tribulations

A worshiping community is crucial, especially during trials and tribulations. The Bible emphasizes the importance of fellowship and community; worshiping with others can provide numerous spiritual and emotional well-being benefits. This section will explore the importance of a worshiping community during trials and tribulations.

1. **The community provides support and encouragement.**

A primary benefit of a worshiping community is the support and encouragement it can provide during difficult times. When we are struggling with adversity, it can be easy to feel isolated or alone. However, being part of a community of believers can offer a sense of connection and belonging and provide a safe space to share our struggles and receive encouragement and support.

For example, a worshiping community can offer prayers, practical support, and emotional comfort when dealing with an illness or loss. This can help alleviate some of the stress and anxiety associated with difficult circumstances and provide hope and assurance.

2. **The community provides accountability and growth.**

Another benefit of having a worshiping community is the accountability and growth it can offer. When we worship with others, we are exposed to different perspectives and experiences, which can help us to grow in our faith and gain new insights into God's character and will. Additionally, community involvement can offer accountability and support to live out our faith and make positive life changes.

For example, a worshiping community can offer Bible study, mentoring, or discipleship opportunities, which can help us grow in our understanding of God's word and apply it to our lives. Additionally, being part of a community can offer support and accountability in relationships, finances, or personal growth.

3. **The community provides a sense of purpose and mission**.

Finally, a worshiping community can provide a sense of purpose and mission, which can be especially important during trials and tribulations. When we worship, we are reminded of our mission to serve God and share His love with others. This can offer a sense of meaning and purpose, even during difficult circumstances.

For example, a worshiping community can offer service, outreach, or evangelism opportunities to help us connect with others and make a difference in our communities. Additionally, being part of a community can offer a sense of purpose and direction in our personal lives, helping us navigate difficult circumstances with hope and determination.

Having a worshiping community is essential during times of trials and tribulations. It can offer support and encouragement, accountability and growth, and a sense of purpose and mission. Being part of a worshiping community allows us to find strength and hope in our faith and connect with others who share our faith journey.

Chapter 3

WORSHIPING GOD IN TIMES OF TRIALS AND TRIBULATIONS

Life is full of ups and downs, and often we face trials and tribulations that can challenge our faith and leave us feeling lost and alone. During these difficult times, worshiping can be a powerful tool for finding comfort, strength, and guidance. This chapter will explore the different forms of worship and how they can be applied during trials and tribulations.

We will also provide steps to worship during difficult times and offer tips on continuing worshiping when the going gets tough. By understanding the different forms of worship and how they can be applied, we can find solace and strength in our faith, knowing that God is always with us, even in the darkest times.

Understanding The Different Forms of Worship

Worship is a crucial aspect of the Christian faith, and it can take many different forms. Understanding the various forms of worship can help us connect with God more meaningfully and find comfort and strength during trials and tribulations. In this section, we will explore some of the different forms of worship and how they can be applied during difficult times.

1. **Praise and Worship**

One of the most common forms of worship is praise and worship. This can be singing worship songs, hymns, or choruses and expressing our gratitude and love for God through music. Praise and worship can be a powerful way to connect with God and find solace and comfort during difficult times.

During times of trials and tribulations, singing praise and worship songs can be a means of finding comfort and strength. When we sing, we can focus our minds and hearts on God's goodness and faithfulness, helping us to feel more grounded in our faith.

2. **Prayer**

Another form of worship is prayer. Prayer involves:
- Speaking to God.
- Sharing our thoughts, feelings, and concerns.

- Asking for His guidance and help.

Prayer can be a means of finding comfort and peace during difficult times, and it can also help us to gain perspective and clarity.

During trials and tribulations, prayer can be a means of finding comfort and guidance. By sharing our concerns with God, we can feel more connected to Him and gain a perspective on our problems. We can also ask for His help and guidance, trusting in His wisdom and love to see us through.

3. **Meditating on God's Word**

Meditation on God's word can be another form of worship that is be helpful during times of trials and tribulations. Meditation involves quieting our minds and focusing on God's word and His presence. It can be a means of finding calm and clarity during difficult times, helping us to connect with God's presence and guidance.

During times of trials and tribulations, meditation can be a means of finding peace and clarity. By focusing on God's presence and peace, we can let go of our worries and concerns and trust in His wisdom and love to guide us.

4. **Bible Study**

Another form of worship is Bible study. This involves reading and studying the Bible and gaining a deeper understanding of God's word and His character. Bible study can be a means of finding guidance, wisdom, and hope during difficult times, helping us trust in God's plan and faithfulness.

Bible study can be a means of finding strength and guidance during trials and tribulations. Reading and studying the Bible, we can better understand God's promises and character, helping us trust His goodness and faithfulness. We can also find comfort and hope in the stories of others who have faced difficult circumstances and found solace in their faith.

5. **Acts of Service**

Acts of service can be a means of finding purpose and meaning during difficult times and expressing our gratitude and love to God. Finally, acts of kindness can also be a form of worship. This involves serving others in our local communities or through mission work and reflecting God's love and compassion through our actions.

During trials and tribulations, acts of service can be a means of finding purpose and meaning. By serving others, we can reflect God's love and compassion and find a sense of purpose in making a difference in the lives of others. We can also find comfort and strength in knowing that we are part of a larger community of believers working together to impact the world positively.

Understanding the different forms of worship can be helpful during times of trials and tribulations. By incorporating other forms of worship into our lives, such as praise and worship, prayer, meditation, Bible study, and acts of service, we can find solace and strength in our faith and connect with God on a deeper level.

Steps To Take To Worship During Trials And Tribulations

As we've discussed previously, worship is an essential aspect of the Christian faith and can be a powerful tool for finding comfort, strength, and guidance during trials and tribulations. However, knowing how to worship effectively can be challenging when facing difficult circumstances. This section will explore some practical steps to worship during trials and tribulations.

1. **Acknowledge your feelings**

The first step in worshiping during trials and tribulations is acknowledging your feelings. It is okay to feel overwhelmed, sad, or angry during difficult times, and it is essential to recognize these emotions before beginning to worship. This can help you to be honest with God and yourself about your struggles and bring them to Him in prayer.

2. **Set aside time for worship.**

The second step in worshiping during trials and tribulations is to set aside time for worship. This could involve setting aside a specific time each day for worship, such as in the morning or before bed. Alternatively, it could include finding time throughout the day to engage in short periods of worship. Finding time to worship during difficult times can be challenging, but it is essential to prioritize it.

3. **Choose a form of worship that resonates with you.**

The third step in worshiping during trials and tribulations is choosing a worship form that resonates with you. There are many different forms of worship, including prayer, meditation, Bible study, singing, and acts of service. Consider which form of worship feels most natural to you and make it a part of your daily routine.

4. **Connect with others**

The fourth step in worshiping during trials and tribulations is to connect with others. Worshiping with others can be a powerful way to find support and encouragement during challenging circumstances. Consider joining a church or small group where you can worship with others and receive prayer and support.

5. **Practice gratitude**

Finally, it is essential to practice gratitude during times of trials and tribulations. Expressing gratitude can help shift your focus away from your problems and toward God's blessings. Consider starting a gratitude journal or taking time each day to reflect on what you are thankful for.

Worship can be a powerful tool for finding comfort, strength, and guidance during trials and tribulations. By acknowledging your feelings, setting aside time for worship, choosing a form that resonates with you, connecting with others, and practicing gratitude, you can worship during difficult times and find hope and solace in your faith.

Tips on How to Continue Worshiping During Difficult Times

Navigating difficult times can be challenging, but maintaining your faith and worship practice can bring solace and support. Here are six practical tips to help you continue worshiping during difficult times, focusing on personal growth and adaptability:

1. **Embrace technology:** Utilize digital platforms to participate in worship services, prayer meetings, or faith-based discussions. Many religious communities offer live-streamed services, podcasts, or recorded sermons that can be accessed online. This can help you stay connected to your faith and find inspiration even when you cannot attend in-person services.
2. **Create a dedicated space for worship:** Designate a specific area in your home for prayer, meditation, or other forms of worship. This space should be free of distractions and filled with items that inspire you spiritually. A dedicated space can cultivate a sense of sacredness and focus during your worship sessions.
3. **Engage in Bible Study and reading uplifting literature:** Delve into the Bible, uplifting literature, or faith-based articles to deepen your understanding of your beliefs and to draw inspiration during challenging times. Reading can offer new perspectives and insights to help you grow spiritually and

maintain your connection to your Christian faith.

4. **Practice mindfulness and gratitude:** Difficult times can make it hard to focus on the positive aspects of life. Integrating mindfulness and gratitude into your daily worship can help you stay grounded and connected to your faith. Spend time each day reflecting on God's blessings upon your life and expressing gratitude for them. This practice can help shift your focus away from adverse circumstances and remind you of the support and love surrounding you.

5. **Seek guidance through prayer and meditation**: Turning to God and strengthening your faith is essential during difficult times. Spend prayer or meditation, asking for clarity, strength, and wisdom from the Holy Spirit. By being open to hearing God's voice, you can find the resilience and hope needed to navigate challenging circumstances.

6. **Adapt your worship practices:** Recognize that your worship routine may need to change during difficult times. Be open to adapting your methods to fit your current situation and emotional state. For example, you might replace group worship with individual prayer. Embracing flexibility and adaptability in your worship practices can help you maintain a strong spiritual connection, even in adversity.

By incorporating these six practical tips into your worship routine, you can continue to nurture your Christian faith and find solace during difficult times.

Chapter 4

BIBLICAL VERSES AND PRAYERS FOR WORSHIPING IN TIMES OF TRIALS AND TRIBULATIONS

During trials and tribulations, it is not uncommon for believers to seek solace and strength in their faith. The Bible, a rich source of divine wisdom and guidance, offers numerous verses and prayers that can provide comfort, encouragement, and inspiration during such challenging times. This chapter aims to equip you with a selection of powerful scriptures and prayers that can aid you in maintaining your spiritual connection and resilience in the face of adversity.

We will present a compilation of <u>biblical</u> verses about worshiping God during difficult times. These verses will remind you of God's persistent presence, love, and support, as well as the transformative power of faith in overcoming life's challenges.

Next, we will explore a collection of prayers tailored to worshiping God during trials and tribulations. These prayers will serve as templates and inspiration for your communion with God, helping you express your thoughts, emotions, and needs as you navigate difficult circumstances.

Finally, we will discuss the importance of memorizing and reciting these verses and prayers as part of your spiritual practice. By internalizing these powerful words, you can readily draw upon their comfort and guidance when faced with adversity. Additionally, reciting these verses and prayers can serve as a form of meditation, helping to center your mind and spirit while deepening your relationship with God.

This chapter will give you the tools to face trials and tribulations with courage, hope, and unwavering faith. By familiarizing yourself with these biblical verses and prayers, you can strengthen your spiritual foundation, enabling you to navigate life's challenges with grace and resilience. Furthermore, incorporating these verses and prayers into your daily worship routine can be a powerful reminder of God's presence and support and the transformative power of faith in overcoming even the most daunting obstacles.

As you journey through this chapter, I encourage you to reflect on the verses and what prayers have to offer. Allow them to inspire and uplift your spirit and deepen your relationship with God.

In times of struggle and uncertainty, the Bible offers a wealth of guidance and encouragement to help believers persevere in their faith.

The following compilation of New King James Version (NKJV) biblical verses focuses on worshiping God during difficult times and serves as a powerful reminder of God's enduring love and support:

1. Psalm 46:1-3 "God is our refuge and strength, a very present help in trouble. Therefore we will not fear, even though the earth be removed, and though the mountains be carried into the midst of the sea; though its waters roar and be troubled, though the mountains shake with its swelling. Selah"
2. Isaiah 41:10 "Fear not, for I am with you; be not dismayed, for I am your God. I will strengthen you, yes, I will help you, I will uphold you with My righteous right hand."
3. Romans 8:28 "And we know that all things work together for good to those who love God, to those who are called according to His purpose."
4. 2 Corinthians 12:9-10 "And He said to me, 'My grace is sufficient for you, for My strength is made perfect in weakness.' Therefore most gladly I will rather boast in my infirmities, that the power of Christ may rest upon me. Therefore I take pleasure in infirmities, in

reproaches, in needs, in persecutions, in distresses, for Christ's sake. For when I am weak, then I am strong."
5. Philippians 4:6-7 "Be anxious for nothing, but in everything by prayer and supplication, with thanksgiving, let your requests be made known to God; and the peace of God, which surpasses all understanding, will guard your hearts and minds through Christ Jesus."
6. James 1:2-4 "My brethren, count it all joy when you fall into various trials, knowing that the testing of your faith produces patience. But let patience have its perfect work, that you may be perfect and complete, lacking nothing."
7. 1 Peter 5:10 "But may the God of all grace, who called us to His eternal glory by Christ Jesus, after you have suffered a while, perfect, establish, strengthen, and settle you."
8. Deuteronomy 31:6 "Be strong and of good courage, do not fear nor be afraid of them; for the Lord your God, He is the One who goes with you. He will not leave you nor forsake you."
9. Joshua 1:9 "Have I not commanded you? Be strong and of good courage; do not be afraid, nor be dismayed, for the Lord your God is with you wherever you go."
10. Psalm 23:4 "Yea, though I walk through the valley of the shadow of death, I will fear no

evil; for You are with me; Your rod and Your staff, they comfort me."
11. Psalm 34:17-18 "The righteous cry out, and the Lord hears, and delivers them out of all their troubles. The Lord is near to those who have a broken heart, and saves such as have a contrite spirit."
12. Psalm 55:22 "Cast your burden on the Lord, and He shall sustain you; He shall never permit the righteous to be moved."
13. Psalm 121:1-2 "I will lift up my eyes to the hills—From whence comes my help? My help comes from the Lord, who made heaven and earth."
14. Proverbs 3:5-6 "Trust in the Lord with all your heart, and lean not on your own understanding; in all your ways acknowledge Him, and He shall direct your paths."
15. Isaiah 40:31 "But those who wait on the Lord shall renew their strength; they shall mount up with wings like eagles, they shall run and not be weary, they shall walk and not faint."
16. Matthew 11:28-30 "Come to Me, all you who labor and are heavy laden, and I will give you rest. Take My yoke upon you and learn from Me, for I am gentle and lowly in heart, and you will find rest for your souls. For My yoke is easy and My burden is light."
17. John 16:33 "These things I have spoken to you, that in Me you may have peace. In the world

you will have tribulation; but be of good cheer, I have overcome the world."
18. Romans 5:3-5 "And not only that, but we also glory in tribulations, knowing that tribulation produces perseverance; and perseverance, character; and character, hope. Now hope does not disappoint, because the love of God has been poured out in our hearts by the Holy Spirit who was given to us."
19. Psalm 9:9-10 "The Lord also will be a refuge for the oppressed, a refuge in times of trouble. And those who know Your Name will put their trust in You; for You, Lord, have not forsaken those who seek You."
20. Psalm 55:22 "Cast your burden on the Lord, and He shall sustain you; He shall never permit the righteous to be moved."

Compilation of Prayers Related To Worshiping God During Difficult Times

In times of hardship and uncertainty, prayer can be a powerful way to find solace, guidance, and strength. The following compilation of prayers is designed to help you connect with God and seek divine support during difficult times:

1. **Prayer for Strength and Comfort:** Heavenly Father, I come before You in this time of

difficulty, seeking Your strength and comfort. Help me to remain steadfast in my faith and trust Your divine plan, even when I don't understand the circumstances. Grant me the courage to face my challenges and the wisdom to learn from them. In Jesus' Name, Amen.
2. **Prayer for Peace and Trust:** Lord, amid my trials, I ask for Your peace that surpasses all understanding. Help me to trust in Your will and to know that You are in control of all things. Grant me the serenity to accept what I cannot change and the faith to believe that You will guide me through this storm. In Jesus' Name, I pray, Amen.
3. **Prayer for Guidance and Protection:** Almighty God, I pray for Your guidance and protection as I navigate through these difficult times. Please show me the path I should take and provide me with the discernment to make the right decisions. Surround me with Your love and shield me from physical and spiritual harm. In Jesus' Name, I pray, Amen.
4. **Prayer for Hope and Healing:** Merciful Father, I come to You for hope and healing. Help me find the strength to persevere through this challenging time and to believe in Your promise of a brighter future. Heal my heart, mind, and soul, and grant me the grace to

trust in Your infinite goodness and love. In Jesus' name, I pray, Amen.

5. **Prayer for Patience and Endurance:** Gracious God, grant me the patience and endurance to face challenges with grace and resilience. Help me to understand that You are working in my life, even when I cannot see it. Teach me to wait on Your perfect timing and to trust in Your divine plan for my life. In Jesus' Name, I pray, Amen.
6. **Prayer for Surrender and Faith:** Lord, during my trials, I surrender my worries, fears, and doubts to You. Help me to release my need for control and to trust in Your sovereignty. Strengthen my faith and remind me that You are always with me, guiding and supporting me through every challenge. In Jesus' Name, I pray, Amen.
7. **Prayer for Wisdom and Discernment:** Heavenly Father, I ask for Your wisdom and discernment as I face this difficult time. Help me to see my situation through Your eyes and to make decisions that align with Your will. Grant me the clarity to recognize Your guidance and the courage to follow Your lead. In Jesus' Name, I pray, Amen.
8. **Prayer for Love and Support:** God of love and compassion, surround me with Your love and support during these challenging times. Fill me with the knowledge that I am never alone, and help me to feel Your presence in my life.

Send caring individuals to provide comfort, encouragement, and assistance as I navigate my trials. In Jesus' Name, I pray, Amen.

9. **Prayer for Courage and Confidence:** Lord, I ask for the courage and confidence to face my struggles head-on. Help me to recognize the strength within myself that comes from You and to trust that I can overcome any obstacle with Your guidance. Remind me to turn to You in every moment of doubt and fear. In Jesus' Name, I pray, Amen.

10. **Prayer for Resilience and Perseverance:** Heavenly Father, in this challenging time, grant me the resilience and perseverance to keep moving forward. When I feel overwhelmed or discouraged, remind me of Your enduring love and the power of my faith. Strengthen my resolve and help me to grow through my trials. In Jesus' Name, I pray, Amen.

11. **Prayer for Grace and Humility:** Almighty God, as I navigate through these difficult times, help me to approach each situation with grace and humility. Teach me to lean on You and to recognize my limitations. Allow me to accept the help of others and extend grace to myself and those around me. In Jesus' Name, I pray, Amen.

12. **Prayer for Acceptance and Understanding:** Merciful Father, grant me the acceptance and understanding I need to face my

challenges with an open heart. Help me to see the purpose behind my trials and to trust that You are using them for my growth and betterment. Allow me to find peace in accepting Your will, even when difficult. In Jesus' Name, I pray, Amen.

13. **Prayer for Joy and Gratitude:** Lord, in my struggles, help me to find joy and gratitude in the blessings You have given me. Teach me to focus on my life's positive aspects and appreciate the gifts surrounding me, even in the darkest times. Fill my heart with Your joy and thankfulness. In Jesus' Name, I pray, Amen.

14. **Prayer for Spiritual Growth and Transformation:** Heavenly Father, I pray that these tough times serve as an opportunity for spiritual growth and transformation. Guide me in my journey towards a deeper relationship with You. Help me to draw closer to You and to learn from my experiences so that I may emerge more potent and more faithful. In Jesus' Name, I pray, Amen.

15. **Prayer for Unity and Fellowship:** Almighty God, in this time of hardship, I pray for unity and fellowship within my community and with fellow believers. Please help us to support one another, share our burdens, and to be a source of strength and encouragement. May our shared faith and collective efforts bring us

closer together and strengthen our bond as we navigate these challenges. In Jesus' Name, I pray, Amen.

These prayers offer a foundation for connecting with God and seeking divine support during difficult times. Feel free to adapt them to your specific needs and circumstances or use them as a starting point for your communion with God.

Explanation of the Importance of Memorizing and Reciting These Verses and Prayers

Memorizing and reciting biblical verses and prayers can be a powerful spiritual practice, particularly during trial and tribulation. Engaging in this discipline can offer numerous benefits, including deepening your faith, providing comfort, and strengthening your resilience. This section will explore the importance of memorizing and reciting these verses and prayers during difficult times.

1. **Internalizing the Word of God:** By memorizing and reciting scripture, you internalize the Word of God, allowing it to become an integral part of your thoughts, beliefs, and actions. This can lead to a deeper understanding of your faith and a stronger connection to God.

2. **Immediate access to comfort and guidance:** When facing challenging situations or experiencing intense emotions, thinking clearly or remembering specific verses and prayers can be difficult. Having these resources memorized enables you to access them instantly, providing immediate comfort, guidance, and encouragement in times of need.
3. **Meditation and reflection:** Reciting verses and prayers can serve as a form of meditation, helping to focus your mind and center your spirit. This practice can help calm anxiety, reduce stress, and promote peace and well-being, even amid turmoil.
4. **Strengthening resilience:** Regularly memorizing and reciting scripture and prayers can strengthen your spiritual resilience, allowing you to draw on these resources to maintain your faith and persevere through adversity.
5. **Nurturing a personal relationship with God:** Memorizing and reciting verses and prayers can help foster a personal relationship with God, facilitating a more intimate and meaningful connection.
6. **Sharing faith with others:** When you memorize verses and prayers, you are better equipped to share your faith with others who may also be facing challenges. Offering these words of

encouragement can provide comfort and support to those in need while fostering a sense of community and fellowship among believers.

7. **Deepening spiritual practice:** Incorporating the memorization and recitation of verses and prayers into your daily spiritual routine can enrich your worship experience, enhance your understanding of scripture, and help you develop a more consistent and fulfilling relationship with God.

Memorizing and reciting biblical verses and prayers can be a valuable spiritual practice, especially during times of difficulty. By integrating this discipline into your daily routine, you can deepen your faith, find solace in times of need, and strengthen your spiritual resilience to face life's challenges with grace and grit.

Chapter 5

EMBRACING WORSHIP DURING DIFFICULT TIMES

As we conclude this exploration into worshiping during difficult times, reflecting on the key insights and spiritual tools presented throughout this journey is essential. This final chapter will recap the importance of worshiping God during trials and tribulations, encourage you to persevere in your faith, and offer final thoughts and recommendations for your spiritual journey.

Recap of the Importance of Worshiping God During Difficult Times:

Worshiping God during difficult times is essential for maintaining a solid spiritual foundation and finding solace in adversity. By turning to God in prayer, meditation, and scripture, you can access divine guidance, comfort, and strength to help you navigate life's challenges. Moreover, embracing worship during hardship can deepen your faith, foster resilience, and serve as a source of inspiration and hope.

Encouragement to Continue Worshiping God During Trials and Tribulations:

It is natural to experience moments of doubt, fear, and uncertainty during trial and tribulation. However, during these challenging moments, the power of worship becomes most evident. As you face life's obstacles, we encourage you to remain steadfast in your worship practice, trusting in God's infinite wisdom, love, and support. By drawing upon your faith and the spiritual resources presented throughout this journey, you can find the courage and resilience to overcome adversity and emerge stronger than before.

Final Thoughts and Recommendations:

In closing, we would like to offer a few final thoughts and recommendations for your spiritual journey:

1. Be flexible and adaptable in your worship practice, adjusting your routine and methods to accommodate your unique needs and circumstances.

2. Maintain a robust spiritual community, connecting with fellow believers for support, encouragement, and fellowship.
3. Continuously seek opportunities for spiritual growth and development, exploring new forms of worship, engaging in self-reflection, and deepening your understanding of scripture.
4. Remember that your spiritual journey is unique, and your worship practices should be tailored to your preferences and experiences.
5. Above all, trust in the power of worship to provide strength, comfort, and guidance during even the most challenging times.

As you continue your faith journey, may you find solace, resilience, and inspiration in your worship practice, allowing the Heavenly Father to guide and support you through life's trials and tribulations.

Bonus Chapter

Worksheets and activities to help you apply the concepts presented in the book. Access the worksheets and journal templates for this chapter by visiting https://www.AndrewMwema.com/downloads.

Or Scan the QR code below;

1. **Bible Verse Memorization Worksheet:**

Objective: Memorize one weekly Bible verse about worshiping God during difficult times.

Instructions:
  I. Choose a verse from the list provided in the book, or select one that resonates with you.
  II. Write the verse in the space provided, along with the date and any personal reflections.
  III. Spend a few minutes each day reciting the verse, and track your progress throughout the week.

Worksheet layout:
- Date:
- Bible Verse:
- Personal Reflection:
- Memorization Progress (circle one): 1 2 3 4 5 6 7 (days)

2. **Prayer Journal:**

Objective: Cultivate a habit of daily prayer during difficult times.

Instructions: Set aside time each day to engage in prayer. Use the space in the journal to write down your prayer requests, thoughts, reflections, and any insights or guidance you may receive during your prayer time.

Journal layout:
- Date:
- Prayer Requests:
- Thoughts and Reflections:
- Insights and Guidance:

3. **Scripture Reflection Activity:**

Objective: Reflect on the meaning of a selected Bible verse and how it applies to your current situation.

Instructions:
  I. Choose a Bible verse from the book or one personally meaningful to you.
  II. Read the verse multiple times and reflect on its meaning.
  III. Write down any insights or personal applications that come to mind.

Worksheet layout:
- Bible Verse:
- Verse Interpretation:
- Personal Application:

4. **Spiritual Growth Goal Setting:**

Objective: Set specific, measurable, achievable, relevant, and time-bound (SMART) goals for your spiritual growth.

Instructions:
  I. Reflect on your spiritual practice and areas where you would like to grow.

II. Set SMART goals for the next month, three, and six months.
III. Revisit your goals periodically to assess your progress and make adjustments as needed.

Worksheet layout:
- One-month SMART goal:
    - Action steps to achieve the goal:
    - Progress check-in date:
- Three-month SMART goal:
    - Action steps to achieve the goal:
    - Progress check-in date:
- Six-month SMART goal:
    - Action steps to achieve the goal:
    - Progress check-in date:

By completing these worksheets and activities, readers can apply the concepts presented in the book to their spiritual journey, helping them grow in faith and resilience during difficult times.

Inspirational Quotes Related to Worshiping God During Difficult Times

1. "When you are going through difficulty and wonder where God is, remember that the teacher is always quiet during a test." - Unknown.

2. "God never said that the journey would be easy, but He did say that the arrival would be worthwhile." – Max Lucado.
3. "The darker the night, the brighter the stars, the deeper the grief, the closer is God!" – Fyodor Dostoevsky
4. "When you pass through the waters, I will be with you; and when you pass through the rivers, they will not sweep over you. When you walk through the fire, you will not be burned; the flames will not set you ablaze." – Isaiah 43:2
5. "Don't tell God how big your storm is; tell the storm how big your God is." – Unknown.
6. "Difficult times are opportunities to better things; they are stepping stones to greater experience. Perhaps someday, you will be thankful for some temporary failure in a particular direction. When one door closes, another always opens." – Brian Adams.
7. "God's plan for your life is happening right now. It doesn't begin when you get married or when you get your dream job, or when everything feels perfect. You are IN the plan." – Lysa TerKeurst.
8. "Faith does not eliminate questions. But faith knows where to take them." – Elisabeth Elliot.
9. "Your hardest times often lead to the greatest moments of your life. Keep going. Tough situations build strong people in the end." – Roy T. Bennett.

10. "In difficult times, always carry something beautiful inside." – Blaise Pascal.

Use these inspirational quotes as a source of encouragement and motivation during difficult times. They serve as reminders that worshiping God during trials and tribulations can bring you closer to God, strengthen your faith, and guide you through the storms of life.

ABOUT THE AUTHOR

Andrew Mwema is a gifted musician whose passion for worship and music sets him apart. With his background as a musician and keyboardist at his local church, Andrew brings a unique perspective and expertise to worship music. As the creator of the Worship Keys TV YouTube Channel, Andrew has created a platform dedicated to helping people create an atmosphere of worship through music.

In addition to his musical gifts, Andrew is also an accomplished entrepreneur and a Maxwell Leadership Certified Coach, Trainer, and Speaker.

His broad range of skills and experience make him well-equipped to lead and inspire others in their spiritual journeys.

Andrew and his wife Veronica are blessed with four wonderful children residing in Houston, TX.

Through Worship Keys TV, Andrew continues to share his gifts and make a positive impact on the lives of others. Whether you're looking for inspiration, comfort, or simply background music for your quiet time, Worship Keys TV is a valuable resource for anyone who seeks to deepen their relationship with God through worship and music.

Scan the QR code to access the Worship Keys TV YouTube channel.

Check out AndrewMwema.Com or scan the QR code below to explore additional publications and resources.

Made in the USA
Middletown, DE
06 May 2023